Modular Design Frameworks

A Projects-based Guide for UI/UX Designers

James Cabrera

Apress®

Modular Design Frameworks: A Projects-based Guide for UI/UX Designers

James Cabrera
Holbrook, New York, USA

ISBN-13 (pbk): 978-1-4842-1687-3   ISBN-13 (electronic): 978-1-4842-1688-0
DOI 10.1007/978-1-4842-1688-0

Library of Congress Control Number: 2017951445

Cover image designed by Freepik

Managing Director: Welmoed Spahr
Editorial Director: Todd Green
Acquisitions Editor: Natalie Pao
Development Editor: James Markham
Technical Reviewer: Massimo Nardone
Coordinating Editor: Jessica Vakili
Copy Editor: Karen Jameson
Compositor: SPi Global
Indexer: SPi Global
Artist: SPi Global

Distributed to the book trade worldwide by Springer Science+Business Media New York, 233 Spring Street, 6th Floor, New York, NY 10013. Phone 1-800-SPRINGER, fax (201) 348-4505, e-mail orders-ny@springer-sbm.com, or visit www.springeronline.com. Apress Media, LLC is a California LLC and the sole member (owner) is Springer Science + Business Media Finance Inc (SSBM Finance Inc). SSBM Finance Inc is a **Delaware** corporation.

For information on translations, please e-mail rights@apress.com, or visit http://www.apress.com/rights-permissions.

Apress titles may be purchased in bulk for academic, corporate, or promotional use. eBook versions and licenses are also available for most titles. For more information, reference our Print and eBook Bulk Sales web page at http://www.apress.com/bulk-sales.

Any source code or other supplementary material referenced by the author in this book is available to readers on GitHub via the book's product page, located at www.apress.com/978-1-4842-1687-3. For more detailed information, please visit http://www.apress.com/source-code.

Printed on acid-free paper

Contents at a Glance

Contents

About the Author

James Cabrera is a self-taught Filipino-American designer based in New York City. With a formal education in Math and Physics, James forged his own path into design, working for companies like Foot Locker, Say Media, and Refinery29 over the past 10 years. His analytical approach unconventional thinking, and knack for problem-solving has greatly contributed to his success. He has also spoken at conferences internationally and frequently writes about his design strategies. James loves constantly learning new things, and sharing knowledge he has acquired over the years. In his free time he is currently focusing on art, photography, and videography.

About the Technical Reviewer

Massimo Nardone has more than 22 years of experience in Security, Web/Mobile development, Cloud, and IT Architecture. His true IT passions are Security and Android.

He has been programming and teaching how to program with Android, Perl, PHP, Java, VB, Python, C/C++, and MySQL for more than 20 years. He holds a Master of Science degree in Computing Science from the University of Salerno, Italy.

Massimo has worked as a Project Manager, Software Engineer, Research Engineer, Chief Security Architect, Information Security Manager, PCI/SCADA Auditor, and Senior Lead IT Security/Cloud/SCADA Architect for many years.

Technical skills include Security, Android, Cloud, Java, MySQL, Drupal, Cobol, Perl, Web and Mobile development, MongoDB, D3, Joomla, Couchbase, C/C++, WebGL, Python, Pro Rails, Django CMS, Jekyll, Scratch, etc.

He currently works as Chief Information Security Officer (CISO) for Cargotec Oyj.

He worked as a visiting lecturer and supervisor for exercises at the Networking Laboratory of the Helsinki University of Technology (Aalto University). He holds four international patents (PKI, SIP, SAML, and Proxy areas).

Massimo has reviewed more than 40 IT books for different publishing companies and he is the coauthor of *Pro Android Games* (Apress, 2015).

This book is dedicated to Antti Jalonen and his family who are always there when I need them.

Introduction

As a digital designer, how often has a project you worked on made it into production 100% as you had designed it? In more cases than not, you may have passed off a deliverable to development only to have many questions exchanged back and forth before eventually getting a link to something that looks quite different than what you originally envisioned.

In the current state of digital design, you almost never truly have a blank slate to work with at the beginning of any project. You're often already binded to a myriad of factors, from needing to use an already chosen premade platform, to the limited capabilities of the people developing your designs.

This book isn't about teaching you how to use one of the many named frameworks already out there. It's for the designer to reshape the way they approach digital design without needing to learn a single line of code. We aim to teach the designer how to structure the way they approach their designs in a way that's conducive to the digital format.

There is a unique property of digital that doesn't exist in any other medium. It is the ability to instantly change the design after it has already been delivered to the user. Being able to really leverage that property alone will add infinite potential to your product.

Interchangeable parts in combination with the assembly line in manufacturing gave rise to the Industrial Revolution. Why? The ability to mass produce identical parts in the creation of a product made it cheaper and easier for a massive amount of people to own and maintain. If you own a car and it breaks down because of the failure of a particular component, there is likely the same component lying around somewhere that you can easily buy and replace the broken one with.

Modular Design has the same exact effect to the success of digital products, if approached in the correct way. This book aims to help guide you on how to design a digital product in a similar way that can be scaled and maintained for the masses. How can you approach your designs in a way that can be easily built in code and easily updateable throughout time? That's what we seek to answer throughout this book.

To continue the car metaphor, we won't be teaching you how to design a clay model of a hypothetical car. We will teach you how to connect a chassis, an engine, tires, and a steering wheel to make a basic functioning car. Everything else you want to put around that is up to you.

CHAPTER 1

A Modular Future

So you need a Modular Design Framework. At least that's the recommendation you've gotten based on an objective analysis of the state of your current product (Figure 1-1).

Figure 1-1. *Have you been in a meeting like this before? (Illustration by Sarah Sabiniano)*

© James Cabrera 2017
J. Cabrera, *Modular Design Frameworks*, DOI 10.1007/978-1-4842-1688-0_1

There have been many case studies done, many books written, and many talks given that explain why you need to have a Modular Design Framework. Being a designer, where do you even begin?

You, as a designer, should feel empowered to take charge when it comes to designing a Modular Design Framework. That means understanding the underlying motivations of why more and more people are employing Modular Design Frameworks. While in doing so we might discover that the shift is developer-centric, it also has unique advantages from a design perspective. The challenge really is in how we can unite the thinking between both designers and developers in order to create great products.

Breaking Down the Buzzword

It's safe to say that "Modular Design Framework" has reached industry buzzword status nowadays. For much of the engineering community, it has become a code word for "use a component library."

Things like Bootstrap, Foundation, React, and Polymer might immediately rise to the forefront of the conversation when talking about Modular Design Frameworks. While these technologies may be used as a foundation to produce your Modular Design Framework, they all already come designed from a developer-centric point of view. To put it simply, these systems are precoded libraries that are capable of completing common and generic tasks that facilitate modern-day, rapid software development.

Some may interpret "Modular Design Framework" as synonymous with some of these component libraries. This should not be the case. That is like always referring to tissues as Kleenex, and *only Kleenex*. When you have a runny nose, you wouldn't let it start dripping until someone can *only* provide Kleenex-branded tissues – all you really require is soft disposable material. In some cases you may even use a handkerchief, which is not considered disposable by many standards. The point is that needing a "Modular Design Framework" does not immediately equate to, "We need to use Bootstrap."

In this book, when we refer to Modular Design Frameworks, we are simply talking about them as a logical system of reusable parts. This also includes defining the interactions between those parts. A successfully crafted Modular Design Framework, in its essence, can live on and be expanded upon without the need for a designer after it is established.

That's not to say that it's the designer's job to make themselves useless. After the framework is created, evolving and iterating on the design language of the system to better serve its users is a never-ending job.

If you consider the English language, all of the words in the dictionary today did not exist upon the inception of the language. New words are created from the constantly repeated usage and improvisation of the current set of words. It organically evolves based on use and transforms into a better and more efficient communication system.

That's ultimately what we want out of designs we create for our products. When we create a design system and implement it, we want to constantly observe how everyone uses it, from our developers using it to our users consuming it. As we notice patterns and trends arise, we want to be able to add new pieces, modify existing ones, or maybe even remove that which is no longer useful.

So when we talk about "Modular Design Frameworks," this is the essence of what we're getting to. We want to make you better at establishing the foundation of a system and language for your designs.

The Shift Toward Design-Led Thinking

As mentioned before, defaulting to using a preexisting component library is always a developer-led decision. It is not a wrong decision by any means; it has many advantages. These libraries have already solved common development pain points when it comes to building apps and have already proven to be portable across various environments. This makes development "faster" in the sense that common problems that may arise are already solved.

The negative result of this path is that you are already establishing a restrictive environment before even allowing yourself to fully understand what your product really needs. As a designer, you are always told to "think outside the box." In this approach you are already forcing yourself inside a "box" that's constrained by capabilities of the library that's chosen.

Companies who go down the path developing entirely on top of another framework end up finding themselves in one of two positions. They either see their product becoming more like everyone else's, or they find themselves heavily restricted in trying new ideas on their product and innovating. Once this is realized, it's when the shift usually occurs to take a more design-led approach. With this comes the unfortunate decision to start all over again – with design at the forefront of decision making.

Why not set the rules to your own game from the start?

It's important to note that the aforementioned examples of popular frameworks, among many others, are the end results of specific companies trying to satisfy their own respective product and user needs. Bootstrap was developed for Twitter, Foundation was made for ZURB projects, React was made for Facebook, and Polymer is used to facilitate Google's own Material Design. All of these companies have come up with their own systems that they've created specifically to handle their own product's challenges.

In the long term, it is not advantageous to retrofit your product into the mold of another (Figure 1-2). You will have your own specific product goals and your own hypotheses you'd like to easily run, test, and adapt over time. There is an extra layer of unnecessary work you would need to do to bridge another product framework with your own product strategy.

Figure 1-2. *Retrofitting one game to play another is not always the best option. (Illustration by Sarah Sabiniano)*

With that being said, already existing, established frameworks should not dictate how you should approach designing whatever product you may be working on. Your primary focus going into any project should be on the users of your product. It should not be based on how to adapt your product to another system for the benefit of developers. It's about adapting your product for the benefit of your users by complementing their specific behaviors. When you create, test, and validate designs against your users, you don't want it to be killed by the mere limitations of a code-based framework made for another product.

Of course there is nothing wrong with opting to use one of these already existing frameworks when it comes to creating proof-of-concepts with a fail-fast and fail-often strategy. However, when you're no longer prototyping and your market position is solidified, that's when you need to begin thinking about designing a more lean, sustainable, and scalable solution to better support and optimize around your own product goals and user needs. That means empowering your product with a Modular Design Framework of its own.

Design and Development: Let's Bridge the Gap

Designers often find themselves in situations where they feel like they are at the mercy of the developer, often sacrificing concepts due to a combination of technical feasibility and deadlines. In reality that should not be the case. When it comes to product creation and iteration, design and development should carry equal weight in the process. Designers should establish the what and the why, while developers determine the can and how.

Designer answers: What are we building and why are we building it?

Developer answers: Can we build this and how will we do it?

One of the most valuable things that can happen at the start of any designer and developer relationship is for each side to have a mutual respect for the other's responsibilities.

Commonly the old way of doing things involves design at the start, then handing off comps to developers who then go off and do the work, only to bring the designers back in the end to make sure things look OK before launch (Figure 1-3).

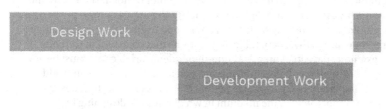

Figure 1-3. *Traditional product development timeline*

More modern processes, like Agile, suggest that both designers and developers have a constant feedback loop throughout the entire process, from inception to launch. Designers focus on the design as the developer is developing it, and they work side by side (Figure 1-4).

Figure 1-4. *Modern product development timeline*

5

I would suggest taking this modern approach slightly further where both designers and developers need to understand the utmost basic logic behind the other's thought processes: in some cases, maybe even contributing to the tasks of the other throughout the entire process (Figure 1-5).

Figure 1-5. Ideal product development timeline

Should Designers Learn to Code?

This brings me to the great debate in recent years over whether or not designers should learn to code. To that question my answer is a resounding No.

Designers should be maximizing their focus on the end users of the products they design. Of course there are many inseparable implications that code has on the core experience. For example, page load time is a code-dependent variable that must be accounted for by the designer. As a designer you can't create designs that would add unreasonable bloat that hinders the overall experience. For reasons like this, designers absolutely need to be empathetic to the medium in which they are designing in.

This is in the same way that an architect needs to understand metal, wood, concrete, or whatever materials need to be used in the buildings they design. Also in the same way an artist effectively adapts their methods and styles based on the composition of paint they are using. Acrylic-, oil-, and water-based paints require completely different techniques from the painter.

The more you understand the medium in which you are designing in, the more seamless it will be for your designs to make it to production as expected. There shouldn't be a constant tug and pull between designer and coder. Designs should be made already with the predictability of how it will be built in code. By designing with an approach that's similar to a coder, you will spend less time figuring out how to make things work and more time figuring out how to iterate and make designs better. Understanding the medium will also allow you to be more creative in finding ways to push it in ways that it's not commonly being used. That's where true creativity and innovation will happen. As a designer it should be your job to bridge the needs of your users with the capabilities of the code.

The best designs are those that are synchronized with the medium.

Design with the Medium

Philosophically, software development is essentially about building a foundation of reusable and componentized code, then iterating on those in order to optimize and build on top of. Oftentimes the best work is seen as that which performs complex tasks in the least amount of lines of code.

As a starting point, it would be advantageous for a designer to align their design thinking with the same approach. This would be much like cutting wood along the grain.

What is the least amount of design we need in order to satisfy our users' needs? What's the best way to reuse those designs in order to optimize the user experience? Are our designs structured in a way that we can repeatedly use them to build more complex applications?

Just by treating design with the same underlying philosophies as the medium we work with, we will be well on our way to establishing our very own frameworks.

The Advantages of Reusability

Reusability of design is not just solely beneficial for the sake of working with the medium. There are also huge advantages of reusing designs from a pure user-experience perspective. By strategically reusing designs, we can create repeatable experiences that will become intuitive over time. Making designs with predictable patterns makes it much easier for your users to find what they need, giving your product a welcoming familiarity.

It's easy to identify what designs can be reused if we look at our elements from a purely functional point of view. Throughout the course of this book, we will be defining every element of our designs by function, which will make it easy for us to determine what we can reuse. If we require elements that need to perform similar tasks, then there's no shame in using things that already exist (Figure 1-6).

Figure 1-6. *If a design already works, there's no reason to change it solely for aesthetic purposes. (Illustration by Sarah Sabiniano)*

The purpose of design, after all, is not just to make things *look different*. Design is meant to solve problems. There is no need to re-create elements that you've already thoughtfully designed and already do the job.

By reusing designs, it will be much easier to gather data and apply updates across the entire system. These are prime opportunities to take advantage of designs that we find to be working effectively and iterate on them to make your entire product better over time.

Iterative Design

If you are consistently reusing elements of design from a functional perspective, you will really see how iteration will consequently be that much easier. In essence it boils down to the idea of designing one to design all. There is an incredible advantage in minimizing duplicative efforts when iterating and improving a single individual element that is repeated across the entire product.

Design should be treated as a constantly evolving system that you can always adapt to changing conditions. It shouldn't be looked at as a disposable layer that can always be scrapped and completely redone at regular intervals. It should be a backbone that you can build a knowledge base on and constantly improve upon.

Taking the Focus Off Aesthetics

While we will be building in a lot of aesthetics into our framework, our goal is ultimately about the design. In this book we want to target your design senses, not your aesthetics. You will learn valuable methods on how to approach establishing your own flexible design system for your products. You also will learn ways to break down an already existing design into a more modular system. In the product development life cycle, design plays a just as, if not more, important of a role as the development. In fact, if your product design strategy is truly user centered, then it should almost always inform the path to development, and not the other way around.

Taking Charge

As you make your way through this book, we will establish the basics of constructing a design that is modular and reusable. We will create a design that works hand in hand with the medium of code. We will also experience designing in an iterative and flexible way, which will allow our designs to grow organically and expand with the needs of our product. Finally, we will focus on the problem-solving attributes of design, decoupling it from its aesthetic quality.

Summary

In this chapter we have defined what a "Modular Design Framework" really means. We have also made the case for why you should learn how to establish a Design Framework of your own entirely from scratch, without relying on something that's already developed. Not only does it afford you more freedom with solutions for your users, but it also makes your product more powerful for iteration and easier to maintain in the long run. With all of this, designers should feel empowered to be part of the crucial decision-making process of how a product will be built.

CHAPTER 2

■ ■ ■

Fonts, Colors, and the Invisible UI

There is a saying, "The best UI is no UI." That seems to be increasingly true as we passively observe the trends in technology. As we continually try to find ways to lower the barriers of friction for our user's adoption of our products, we begin to see more and more of our available UI options disappearing. In the coming years, will there be any space left for design?

Designers are now embracing the need to become minimalists when they're tasked to design digital products — boiling functionality down to its essence. What is the bare minimum you need to have a usable product? Font and color play a more important role now than ever if you're lucky enough to still get a choice in the matter.

Defining Visual Hierarchy

Before doing any design whatsoever, the first thing you need to think about is how you want to prioritize the visual hierarchy. What elements of visual design will you use to cue your users as to what's most important? The elements we will be focusing on for the purposes of this book are size, color, and order.

- Size — The bigger something is, the more important it is.

- Color — Creating primary, secondary, tertiary colors, and fixing them on a scale of importance: that is, always using a primary color on the most important elements.

- Natural Order — Whatever you place first in the natural flow of the document is the most important. Natural flow is subjective based on design. It could be top-down, left-right, outside-inside, etc.

Of course, you are not limited to these options. These are mainly considered in designing for the Web. Depending on what you're designing for, you may have access to even more properties.

© James Cabrera 2017
J. Cabrera, *Modular Design Frameworks*, DOI 10.1007/978-1-4842-1688-0_2

To see a little bit more about how we can leverage the possibilities, let's take a look at a design of an individual tweet on Twitter in Figure 2-1.

James Cabrera
@jamescabrera
Not sure if shower or air conditioner fluid.
#nycproblems
3:48 PM - 27 Jun 2016

Figure 2-1. *This is the actual design of a tweet as seen on Twitter*

By looking at all of the individual elements in this single tweet, what would you think is the most important part of the design? There are actually several different ways to look at it.

A common ordering of importance based on an observed visual hierarchy may go as follows:

- The 140-character Tweet
- The User (name + avatar)
- Actions to take on the tweet
- Data about when the tweet was made

Based on this analysis one might assume the designer thought about establishing the visual hierarchy in the original order I set forth:

- Size
- Color
- Natural Order

But how could this be designed differently if we restructure the visual hierarchy? Say, for example, this is how we wanted to set our priorities:

- Natural Order
- Size
- Color

Figure 2-2 shows a possible design direction. If we want our design framework to value Natural Order the most, then what's most important should come first in the normal flow of reading (in this case top-down, but it could also mean from left to right). In this example, our intention is for the tweet to be most important, followed by the person who said it, then the actions, and lastly when it was posted.

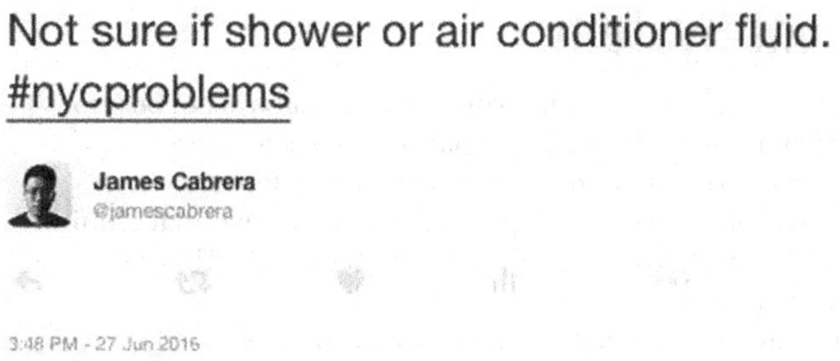

Not sure if shower or air conditioner fluid. #nycproblems

James Cabrera
@jamescabrera

3:48 PM - 27 Jun 2015

Figure 2-2. *Here, the tweet is most important*

Figure 2-3 shows another example using the following hierarchy:

- Color
- Size
- Natural Order

James Cabrera
@jamescabrera

Not sure if shower or air conditioner fluid. #nycproblems

3:48 PM - 27 Jun 2015

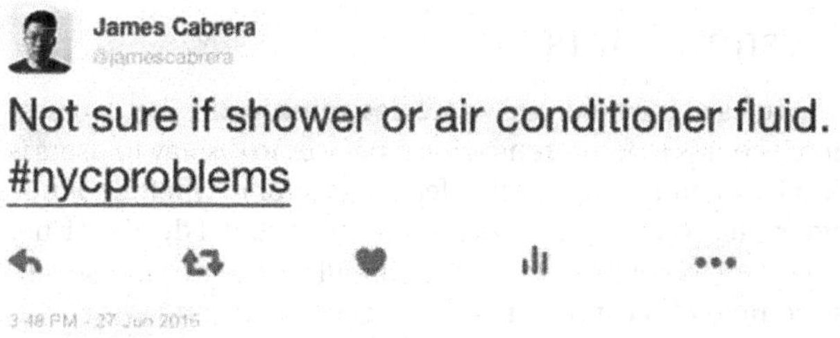

Figure 2-3. *Color, size, natural order*

There is no right or wrong way to establish visual hierarchy. Aesthetically, I wouldn't qualify these designs as the best in the world. The design is ultimately up to you and your users.

The point is that setting up a rule for visual hierarchy and sticking to it consistently throughout your design is a very valuable thing to think about before beginning. We will heavily leverage visual hierarchy to create a design that's purely based on font and color.

For the rest of the examples throughout the rest of this book, this will be the foundation for visual hierarchy we will be operating under:

- Size
- Color
- Natural Order

Establishing a Font System

Let's get started defining a font system for our framework. This section will not be about where to use serif or san-serif fonts, nor will it be about pairing typefaces. We want to build a robust system that's focused on function. With a good enough font system in place, we could theoretically swap font-faces at any point in the process without requiring a major design overhaul. It could be as easy as simply changing a variable. That's the type of system we want to create for our designs.

You might find yourself in one of two situations with respect to fonts.

1. You are designing something brand new. You have a clean slate with respect to choosing fonts.

2. You are designing an interface for a brand that already has well-defined brand guidelines. You need to establish a system that accommodates set font guidelines.

Regardless of which situation you're in, you should always be wary of the limitations of the Web and always communicate them clearly with brand stakeholders.

Custom Fonts and System Fonts

Of course we need to play by the rules of the medium we are designing in, the Web, so we do have a few limitations. When it comes to fonts, rendering typefaces to display to users is a major limitation. A matter of milliseconds could be the deciding factor in whether or not a user stays or bounces from your site. You can have a beautiful design, but if the user isn't willing to wait to see it, then what's the point? We need to be careful in how we choose our fonts. When do we need to use completely custom fonts versus generic system fonts?

We all know the advantage of using custom fonts is that it gives our sites a unique identity. You want to be able to separate yourself, identity-wise, from the rest of the noise of the Internet. The downfall of that is that in order for the user to see such custom fonts, they need to download that extra data in order to see it. That means longer load times since font files are typically not small by web file size standards.

System Fonts, on the other hand, are generic fonts that are already installed on most computers by default, and don't need to be downloaded to be seen. You can save a lot of time by using common system fonts such as Helvetica, Arial, Georgia, and Times New Roman.

The reliance on system fonts is becoming even more and more important with the rise of content distribution platforms where you may have extremely limited control over your design. Examples of content distribution platforms are Facebook Instant Articles, Apple News, Google AMP, and Snapchat Discover. If you plan on distributing your product through these channels, utilizing system fonts becomes of utmost importance in order to maintain the visual consistency of your brand. You don't want your users to have different visual experiences of your designs within each of these different channels, in addition to your own site.

Imagine a user reading a piece of your content on Facebook Instant Articles, then clicking on a link within that article that directs them to a web view of your site. Will there be consistency in the experience? What if you need to spin up a Google AMP version of your content so you can land higher on Google Search results? Wouldn't you want the AMP version of your content to have the same look and feel as the content on your own site? Ideally we would want to maintain visual continuity wherever our user is experiencing our products.

Think About Function Before Form

When defining what fonts we want to use where, we want to always make sure we are defining them based on function over form. What does that mean?

It is a common practice in web development to name fonts under a system in the following way:

```
$serif_font: Georgia, serif;
$sans-serif_font: Arial, sans-serif;
```

This is also a different method with essentially the same fundamental flaw:

```
$primary_font: 'Helvetica Neue', sans-serif;
$secondary_font: Garamond, serif;
```

What's the flaw? These naming techniques define fonts based on form first over function, because the fonts are established on the basis of what the typeface is versus what its function is. Why is this a problem? The typeface is what may be variable as time goes on due to branding changes or other reasons. This defeats the purpose of declaring them as variables to begin with.

So what might stay constant? Defining fonts by their function. In our system we want to think about what types of information we will be commonly communicating with our users, and defining our font system based off of that.

```
$title_font: 'Helvetica Neue', sans-serif;
$subtitle_font: Garamond, serif;
$body_font: Georgia, serif;
```

Figures 2-4 and 2-5 show popular websites and apps, and how they might have defined their fonts based on our proposed naming convention.

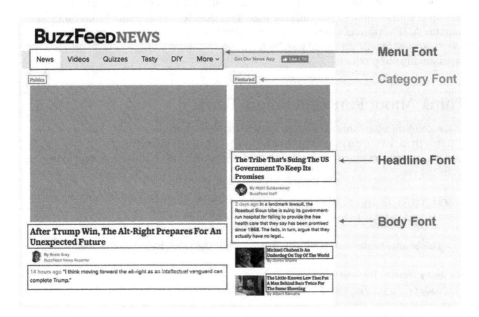

Figure 2-4. *Breaking up the fonts on Buzzfeed News Page by what their functions are versus by the style of the typefaces*

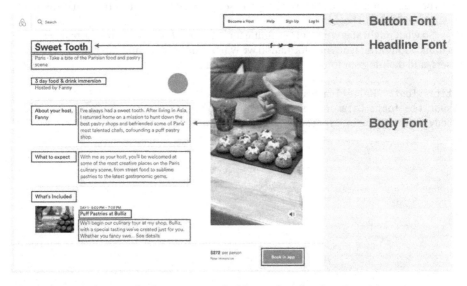

Figure 2-5. *Breaking up the fonts on an Airbnb listing by what their functions are versus by the style of the typefaces*

Establishing a Color System

Creating a color system is a less complicated, more subjective process — but should still be carefully thought out. As a point of emphasis when it comes to usability, you should try not to lean on color too much as an element that defines actions.

Accessibility is the main point of concern. About 4.5% of the world population has some form of color blindness, so we should be extra careful not to bias against or exclude those potential users of our products.

For this reason it is always very useful to think about using tints and taking advantage of contras first, then applying color afterward as an accent.

I almost always recommend looking at color in user interfaces as optional. After all, your content should be the element providing color, and you wouldn't want unexpected combinations of color creating unpleasant visual dissonance. This is also reason to leverage some neutral colors in your palette.

When setting colors for your interface, another important thing to always keep in mind is common color associations. An example of this in UX design is applying color to positive and negative actions, such as saving and deleting. It would be counterintuitive to use a shade of green as a button color for deleting data or cancelling an action. Similarly it may not be the best idea to apply a shade of red for actions like saving progress or submitting data. These types of choices can cause confusion for your users.

For each color, also make sure to consider a corresponding foreground color. There may be instances where your color may be applied as a background where you want text or other elements to sit on top of.

As far as naming goes, it would be beneficial to abstract the names of the colors we would like to use and define them by their roles versus outright calling them by their color name. Consider utilizing a naming system like the following:

- Primary
- Secondary
- Background
- UI

Many people define their colors in their code by their names:

```
$DarkBlue = #0a62e5
```

I advise against this because you may very well in the future need to update your colors. If you no longer wish to use Dark Blue, then you not only have to update the Hex value, but you also need to refactor every spot where your $DarkBlue variable is declared. This sort of defeats the purpose of even using a variable for your colors. Having an abstract color naming system is more scalable to maintain and easy to pivot in case of brand updates.

Let's Design an Example

Now that we have a very basic foundation of visual hierarchy, font, and color, let's try to go through an example of building a pure text- and color-based site design.

In this example, let's build ourselves a simple Nameplate Site. A Nameplate Site is essentially just a site that identifies who you are and has some very basic information about you. It's basically like a business card on the Web.

There are some services that easily allow you to create a Nameplate Site without any coding knowledge whatsoever. The most popular example is about.me (`https://about.me/`).

Let's design our own highly functional Nameplate Site from scratch using what we've learned in this chapter.

The first thing we want to do is decide how we want our visual hierarchy to be defined. In this example, let's go with the following rule of law:

- Size - The biggest things will always be most important.

- Color - Color will be a secondary way to command attention.

- Natural Order - From top to bottom in the document, although not as important as size. For example, a colored element lower in the document might be more important than something small in the beginning.

For fonts, let's start off by using system fonts, then later enhance our design by converting them to custom fonts. Let's think about what information we may want to include in our Nameplate Site, and define our fonts accordingly. Here is some information we might want to include in our design:

- Your name

- Your current title

- Short description about yourself

- Links to your social networks and email address

Considering that, here's how we might want to define our font system:

- Title Font

- Subtitle Font

- Description Font

- Link Font

Choosing this font system doesn't necessarily mean we need to choose four different fonts. Depending on your knowledge of font pairing, typography, and personal style (the subjective aspects), you may choose fewer font families but use them multiple times across your font system.

For this example, let's arbitrarily choose our fonts in the following way.

```
@mixin title_font{
        font-family: Georgia, Garamond, serif;
        letter-spacing: -0.04em;
}
@mixin subtitle_font{
font-family: Arial, Verdana, sans-serif;
font-weight: bold;
}
@mixin description_font{
        font-family: Arial, Verdana, sans-serif;
}
@mixin link_font{
        font-family: Arial, Verdana, sans-serif;
        font-weight: bold;
        text-transform: uppercase;
}
```

Figure 2-6 shows how we would approach designing something as simple as a Nameplate Site. Yes, simple in concept, but with an underlying design strategy behind it makes it a strong foundation to evolve on top of.

James Cabrera

Interface Designer

James Cabrera is a self-taught UI/UX Designer based in New York City. With a degree in Math and Physics, James forged his own path into design. Starting out working for small SEO-based businesses, James eventually went on to work for companies like Foot Locker, Inc and Say Media. He is currently working with Re-finery29, where he has been during the past 2 years, helping to build and define new UX initiatives.

TWITTER · INSTAGRAM · DRIBBBLE · BEHANCE · LINKEDIN

Figure 2-6. *A simple font system and casual hierarchy*

Wearables and Conversational UI

With the advent of smart watches, the rise of conversational UI's, and even the early signs of experimentation in the space of Augmented Reality, we can already start to see the landscape of where our digital products may need to migrate in the coming years. What will be our options for interfacing with users in the next generation of digital platforms?

In the space of smartwatches the majority of the interface is just font and color. There, of course, is very limited real estate to incorporate graphical elements. Even still, any graphical opportunities would have to recede to the text, which will be the main communicator in the interface.

Conversational UI is even tougher. These interfaces often live totally within the environment of another application. From SMS, to Facebook Messenger, and WhatsApp, you don't even have an option to design the text. Take it even further by considering Conversational UI's like Amazon Echo and the impending Google Home. In these cases there is no text. You have but just a voice.

Voice and Tone is often an overlooked aspect of UI design. It also is just the beginning of how we really start considerately designing for what I refer to as the Invisible UI.

Summary

In this chapter we learned how to begin a design from scratch, only relying on the most basic visual devices of visual hierarchy, fonts, and colors. These basic elements are often the very first things you should be thinking about when you approach starting a new design from scratch.

In addition to that, if you are trying to take an existing design and establish a design framework from it, you'll most certainly want to tackle defining visual hierarchy rules, establishing a font and color system first.

Technically once you've established these basic principles, you need to have the utmost minimum knowledge required to start creating logical designs. There are actually plenty of sites out there made with typography alone. Being able to perfect this is true minimalism at its finest.

As we progress through the next few chapters we will be adding additional layers of complexity to how we start grouping and clustering these visual elements. As the content of subjects that we need to design for becomes more elaborate, such as in applications or very large databases, the design framework we are establishing will also need to be more accommodating.

CHAPTER 3

■ ■ ■

Defining Your Basic Unit

Now that we've made decisions around our fonts, colors, and general hierarchy principles, it's time to do some actual design. Design always begins at the essence of your product. That means getting down to the bottom of whatever it is you're trying to accomplish, and figuring out what pieces you need to put together to achieve that goal.

In this chapter we are going to understand the essence of what a basic unit should be by analyzing examples, learn a process on how we can architect our own basic unit, and then go through a practical example – essentially forming the basis of a Modular Design Framework.

Our entire design is going to revolve around how we decide to construct our basic unit. By the end of this chapter we will pretty much have the foundation of a usable product. Although the aesthetic itself may appear very monotonous, it will still be shippable.

Understanding the Essence of Your Product

Design should always be working to facilitate a primary function. What is it that you are trying to accomplish?

- Are you selling a product?
- Are you providing a service?
- Are you presenting information?

After you figure out that question, you must then think about the tangible elements you need that will help you satisfy that goal.

We Need a Product to Sell

What resource does our service come from?

What is the actual piece of information that you want to present?

Whenever you start a design, it's easy to get caught up in the broad idea of what you want to accomplish without thinking about the smallest pieces that will be doing the heavy lifting to get you there.

J. Cabrera, *Modular Design Frameworks*, DOI 10.1007/978-1-4842-1688-0_3

We sometimes get too wrapped up in thinking about things such as increasing sales, acquiring users, or driving views. That's just the bottom line though. Designers need to be focusing on the means of getting there. This starts by discovering what the bare minimum elements you need to have in order to accomplish your task. Thereafter it's all about iterating on that element to hopefully optimize toward your goal.

The theory behind this approach is that once you determine your basic unit, all other UI necessary from there has to do with the manipulation and interactions with that element.

Theory in Practice

In order to better understand the logic behind what I'm proposing, it's always good to go through a few examples. Here I will analyze the designs of a few well-known and widely used products, and under the lens of this approach identify what that product's basic unit can be.

To be clear, I am not saying this is how these products were designed – but only if we were to reimagine their systems if they were to be thought through by using this principle.

Facebook

There seems to be a lot going on design-wise on Facebook; however, it is all based on their basic unit of user posts. These units carry through to Pages, Groups, Events, News, and even Messages (Figure 3-1).

Figure 3-1. *Facebook may seem like an extremely complicated system, but it can really be boiled down into a single basic unit: the individual post*

All of the interactions around Facebook rely heavily on the organization of individual posts, whether that is posts you make, your friends make, or a company makes. The Newsfeed is just an aggregation of posts of all the people you follow. Your "wall" is just an aggregation of all of the individual posts you made. Most of the core functionality of the site happens within each post (reactions, comments, consumption), and also as different ways of aggregating groupings of individual posts.

Airbnb

Airbnb, the popular service that allows you to stay in other people's homes while visiting other cities, can also be reduced down to a single basic unit: individual home listings (Figure 3-2).

Figure 3-2. *With Airbnb, every feature is built around an individual home listing*

Many people may believe that services or utility-driven sites are more abstract than other digital products. But they, too, can be contextualized into basic fundamental units. Even when you consider the UI of the map, it is just merely a different method of aggregating the basic unit.

Uber

Just looking at the interface of Uber, the popular ride-hailing app, it might not be immediately clear what their basic unit could be. However, it could be said that their entire app revolves around each individual driver, represented as cars on a map. Users interact with this basic element of the car representing each driver (Figure 3-3). They are categorized by tiers (uberX, uberBLACK, uberPOOL etc.), and when the user ultimately summons one, they continue to follow that unit through the design on the app until they reach their final destination.

Figure 3-3. Uber's interface revolves around cars, which represent drivers as a basic unit

Amazon

Amazon, like all retailers or shopping-focused sites, has the clear basic unit of a shoppable product (Figure 3-4). The entire design for these types of sites is meant to group and filter a variety of individual products together in different ways.

Figure 3-4. *Individual products are the basic unit for Amazon*

BuzzFeed

BuzzFeed, like many other news and media sites, presents pieces of content to their users as their most basic unit (Figure 3-5). The various pages that make up the site are merely different collections of this basic unit, which can be written content, images, and also video.

Figure 3-5. *BuzzFeed's basic unit is each individual piece of content, represented in discrete blocks*

Chase

Let's look at something a little less obvious – a banking site – through the new updated Chase account page (Figure 3-6).

Figure 3-6. *Chase account page*

You might assume that the company goals for Chase are to acquire accounts and increase investments. Although that's the goal, it doesn't give you any context for the actual elements you need to design for. It may not have any direct relation to how you would need to design an account management page.

If you think more about the essence of the functionality of a banking site, you'll begin to understand what you need to design for. I propose that the basic unit of a banking site would be individual transactions.

Everything that a user would need to do within a banking app involves transactions. Whether that's paying for something, depositing money, transferring, or withdrawing money, every action is just an aspect of individual transactions.

Onward Inward

Once you determine what your basic unit should be, the next task is to start designing the unit itself. Designing inward means determining what elements you need to contain within your unit. Designing outward means determining how you would like to aggregate your basic units across pages. Designing outward also requires figuring out how you want your units to be manipulated.

Since this chapter is about the basic unit, we will focus on how to design inward. In later chapters we will tackle how to build up and out using this unit.

Inventory

The first part of designing the inner part of your basic unit is determining what elements you should display. You don't have to display everything, just enough to give the user relevant context. What you decide to start with will not be set in stone. In coming up with a design, you should keep in mind how you might want to be able to add or remove elements within your unit.

The first thing we want to do is try to take an inventory of everything that we can show. Let's take the example of a piece of content. This could potentially be all of the possible elements you can show in your unit.

- Title of Content

- Short Description

- Image

- Timestamp

- Author

- Tags

- Category

Of course there could me more, depending on what data you actually have. Once you have this inventory, the next step is to start narrowing it down to what you feel is most important. In some cases you may feel that everything is important, but remember, displaying too much information at once could be overwhelming.

Establish a threshold for yourself (I recommend 3-4 elements). Focus on what pieces will represent your unit the best. The point of this unit is to lead the user into a more detailed view.

Flow

The next thing to think about is flow. Think about how you want your units to flow throughout your pages. The most common patterns are the "Z" and "F" patterns (Figure 3-7). However, you may come up with something completely different – you are the designer after all.

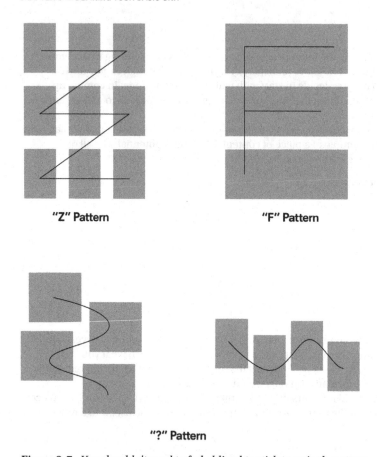

"Z" Pattern   "F" Pattern

"?" Pattern

Figure 3-7. You shouldn't need to feel obliged to stick to a single pattern

You may find that certain pages need different patterns. We will tackle those questions in the next chapter as we focus on designing outward. We just need to have a general idea of where we want to go now as we design the unit itself.

Design

Using your established font, color, and hierarchy principles from the previous chapter, you can take your chosen inventory of elements and your idea of how you might want your units to flow in order to design your unit. This is where you can flex your aesthetic muscles. But don't fall in love with a particular design nor get too perfectionist about it. This will likely change down the road as you will see in a later chapter.

One for All

It's important to note that in the way we are building this modular system, to start, is by using a single unit and repeating it. You may be thinking this is super restrictive and limiting. However, this is the bare minimum you will need to build your product.

Of course there are an infinite amount of use cases you must probably be pouring over in your head, and also a thirst for variety. When it comes to building a functional product, these things are often unnecessary, and merely nice to have. It is possible to move on to the next chapter from here once you decide on the design of your basic unit.

In Chapter 5 we will talk more about testing, iteration, and variation, where we will be able to expand and grow the variety of our designs to accommodate more "types" of content as well as revisit and optimize our designs.

For now, let's go through the practice of designing a basic unit for our current example site.

Building Our Own

As a designer, if we want to do a little more marketing for ourselves above just a basic nameplate site that just has personal details, what would we do next? We might want to make a site that shows several projects that we've worked on. Let's build a portfolio site.

The Basic Unit for our portfolio site will be each individual project that we want to showcase. Our site will be based off of reusing the design we make for this single base unit.

Now let's take an inventory of all the information we want to include in our basic unit and prioritize them based on importance. What you decide you want to include and how you rank each piece of information may differ from the below, but it's all up to you what you decide to show and how.

- Image
- Project Title
- Short Description
- Project Type (i.e., Website, Photography, Graphic Design, etc.)
- Client

As for flow, let's go with a Z pattern for this example (Figure 3-8). We will do a second example afterward to see how an F pattern might look different.

"Z" Pattern

Figure 3-8. For this example, we decide on a Z pattern, which will affect how we design our basic unit

Now that we have decided on all of those details, let's start designing a wireframe of our basic unit design. Let's apply what we learned in Chapter 2 about Fonts, Colors, and Visual Hierarchy.

Here's how we'll establish visual hierarchy:

- Size

- Natural order (top-down)

- Color

Here is the font system we will be using based on our inventory:

- Title Font

- Description Font

- Meta Info Font

Figures 3-9 and 3-10 show two potential designs we could do, but of course the options are unlimited.

Figure 3-9. *One way we can design our unit*

Figure 3-10. *Another take on our basic unit. Aesthetically it can look any way you choose, as long as you accommodate all the elements in your inventory*

Putting them into our decided Z pattern flow would render a site design like that shown in Figure 3-11.

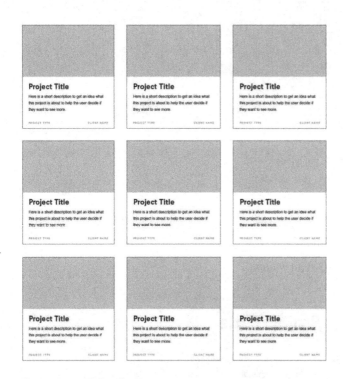

Figure 3-11. *Using the Z pattern*

Figure 3-12 shows what a very basic structure of our design created from our single basic unit will look like.

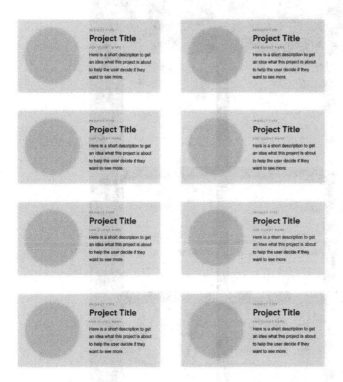

Figure 3-12. *How the same design transforms by using a different basic unit design*

Although these designs may not look like anything groundbreaking, it serves as the foundation for something that can be expanded upon to create something scalable, as you will see in later chapters.

The important thing to note is that with very minimal effort and design, we actually have a shippable product. Let's choose one of the wireframe directions and flesh it out into an actual design with real content (Figure 3-13).

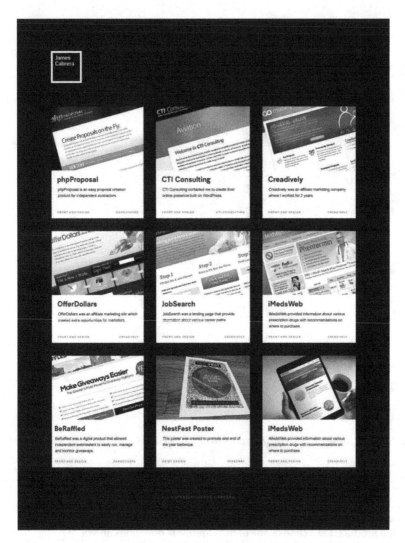

Figure 3-13. The same design with some visual design applied to it

If we had chosen to go with an F pattern, we may approach designing our basic unit differently (Figure 3-14).

Figure 3-14. The basic unit designed for a different flow. Here we consider an F pattern.

Figure 3-15 would be the rendered design in an F pattern that is guided by our unit.

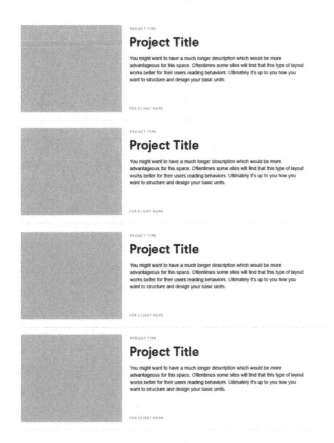

Figure 3-15. How our alternative basic unit design flows for an F pattern

Now that we know the basics of designing a basic unit, we can start thinking about expanding our design by establishing some organization around our units through programming, pages, and navigation.

Summary

In this chapter we defined what a basic unit should be. This is the most important foundational element of your Modular Design Framework. In analyzing your own product, you should be able to identify what you want your basic unit to represent. From there, you should be creating and constantly maintaining an inventory of properties you want to represent your basic unit to your users. This is what you'll have to work with to design. From there, aesthetics is entirely up to you. By focusing on the design of your basic unit, you will indirectly already be designing the rest of your product.

From here, the rest of your framework will depend on establishing logic around variations of your basic unit and also how you want to group your units for different pages.

CHAPTER 4

■ ■ ■

Adaptation, Reusability, Variation, and Iteration

Fold up a piece of paper several times, cut a few holes into the fold, and you have completed a common exercise for elementary schoolchildren. You've made a unique pattern for a snowflake. While this took minimal to no effort at all, you might be surprised to know that – in a class of 30 children – no two snowflakes are the same. If you use a big enough piece of paper and vary the individual shapes you cut into your paper, you might produce some very fascinating designs.

This is essentially why creating a design pattern is so lucrative, especially for bigger businesses. The focus is on designing a small finite set of pieces, yet affecting a much larger, seemingly infinite picture.

This is the approach we want to take with our basic unit. At this point we have designed only a single shape for our design as a whole. On a bigger scale, our single module framework may appear uniform, monotone, and bland.

While this is true, there is also a huge advantage to taking this route for design frameworks. We are able to design and ship a product very quickly. All the work you had to do up to now was to identify and design your basic unit, which is often the core of what your product is.

Just by having this one basic unit design along with your fonts, colors, and visual hierarchy, you can build a quick, minimum viable product with a design system that you can start closing a feedback loop on through actual usage. Being able to start collecting data on your designs early in the process can help better inform the direction of your designs.

The main point of using a Modular Design Framework is to enable our design to evolve with our product. This uniform, monotone, single-unit system is not where the design ends. We can now start collecting data about our design early on, be able to modify it rapidly, and also add units based on new features and extend the performance of our product.

As we learn more about what is resonating with our users, we will get better at knowing exactly what we should add, subtract, and modify versus making guesses and doing the work – only to throw it away.

© James Cabrera 2017

J. Cabrera, *Modular Design Frameworks*, DOI 10.1007/978-1-4842-1688-0_4

Imagine spending months trying to design the perfect ice cream sundae. You carefully plan it out and meticulously choose the ingredients, mixing textures of crunchy and soft, and balancing the savory and sweet. Once you present this sundae to your primary user, you find out they don't like chocolate. Meanwhile, several of the ingredients you used on this sundae have chocolate in it and you need to go back to the beginning to make a new sundae without chocolate.

It would have been nice to know this early on in this process: having tried serving your user a basic scoop of chocolate ice cream first, then trying out individual ingredients one at a time to see how your user responds to them – before you start pairing complex textures and flavors.

This chapter will guide us through how we handle that same exact process of trying out different ingredients to find a design that works well for our users.

Preventing Confirmation Bias in Design

There is no crystal ball that will outline *all* of the elements you will need to create designs for at the beginning of any project. Much of the beginning is just a lot of guesswork based on past experiences and the imitation of products that are already out there. This is a potential minefield of confirmation biases that can do harm to your users, or even exclude users.

One of the biggest flaws when it comes to design is the assumption that our own preferences will be the same as those of our users.

"I love chocolate, so how could anyone hate chocolate?"

This type of thinking may cause us to only focus on results that prove our assumptions, or only seek feedback from others who share similar opinions. When we allow little biases like this to add up before closing the loop with our actual users, it may hurt our designs in the long run. We invest and waste a lot of energy in something that could have been proven wrong early on.

The real design work that will have a meaningful impact on your product happens after a product is launched and you analyze how it gets used to determine what it needs.

This is a great reason for designers to be more comfortable shipping basic elements first, then building on our design systems from there, armed with better data.

How to Adapt What You Have

So how do you approach taking what you have, and evolving it to be better at handling more complex tasks for your product? In approaching developing our Modular Design Framework, we want to create a plan for how we introduce different designs for our basic unit, so we don't go out of control assuming we need to create a new design for anything and everything that comes up.

Remember we want to keep our framework as lean as possible: a smaller finite pool of modules based on our basic unit that we can easily maintain. In Figure 4-1 we show a line of questioning we need to apply to how we approach introducing new designs. This is our playbook for adapting our framework.

Can we reuse a design
we already have?

Can we make simple
modifications to a
design we already have?

Can we add a feature to a
design we already have?

We need a new design.

Figure 4-1. *The line of questioning we need to ask ourselves before introducing any new design to our framework*

Our last course of action should be requiring a new design. Since we want to create a sustainable design framework, we should make every effort to use what we already have and build upon it. This is crucial to the success of our Modular Design Framework.

Recycling and Reusing Basic Units

In our design method, our first course of action is to extend the capabilities of what we already have. How do you make do with what you already have to meet the needs of something new that you want to accomplish? Answering this question will be your greatest task as the architect of your design framework.

Figure 4-2 shows the basic unit that we designed in our previous chapter.

Figure 4-2. *A basic unit design from the previous chapter*

This unit was designed to represent a project as part of a portfolio. However, say, for example, we want to now also include bits of information about ourselves on the same page. Instead of going right ahead and designing a brand new unit, let us think instead about adapting our current unit (Figure 4-3).

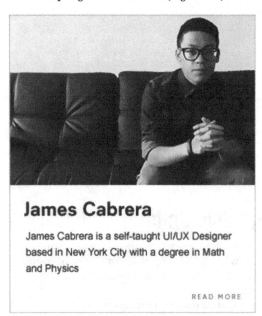

Figure 4-3. *Repurposing the basic unit made to represent a project to now represent a person who has different data types of data*

If you find that the design that you went with is not adequate to meet your needs, you can adapt the design to meet the needs of both your current and your new features (Figure 4-4).

Hello There!

My name is James and I am an award-winning User Experience and Interface Designer based in New York.

NestFest

This poster was created to promote an end of the year barbeque.

Figure 4-4. After seeing how a person looks in this card format, you may want to update the design of your basic unit to something that can display both types of content better

Whenever you encounter needing to add something new to your framework, see if you can use any of your current designs to represent the new information. Try first to do a straight replacement of the content. If it works, then consider whether or not you want to update the design of your basic unit to better accommodate the new context you need to use it for.

Variation

If attempting to reuse an element fails to accommodate different use cases you need to satisfy, then you may begin introducing variations of your units. Variations are just simple modifications to an existing design to accommodate different needs. For the most part, a variation retains much of the same design qualities with a slight tweak in only a few variables. We will go through a couple of examples that exemplify how we implement variations to our basic unit design.

Example: Size

An example of a type of variation we might want to introduce is on the size of our units. Maybe certain pieces of content are more important to us than others. In the example of my portfolio, I feel my website work is stronger and more in depth than my print pieces, so I want my design to communicate that to the user. A simple way to accommodate this use case is to apply a size variation to my unit design for when they accommodate websites.

In Figure 4-5 notice how all of the attributes of the modules remain the same except for the size of the width. Variation is most easily implemented with the minimum amount of attributes changed. Think of ways to leverage simple changes in order to maintain a familiar visual system.

Figure 4-5. *Applying a size variation to my basic unit design for websites*

Example: Availability of Data

We might want to create variations in our modules for the reason of availability of data. What does that mean?

In our example, we designed our module to have an image, headline, description text, and call-to-action to view the project. What if a particular piece of data we want to use our module design for doesn't have an image?

We might want to consider variations in our module design that excludes missing data. In many cases the design may not work by just simply leaving out an element, and we need to make additional tweaks to the design to fill the void. So maybe for elements that don't have an image, we need to bump up the font size of the headline.

In Figure 4-6 we show this third variation on the basic unit for a card representing a written article titled, "Do It Right, or Do It Twice."

Figure 4-6. *Showing a third basic unit variation to represent an article that doesn't have an associated image attached to it*

Taking It Further

These are just very basic use cases for how we implement simple variations. How you determine variations for your framework is entirely up to you. You may want to establish logic to have modules be different colors than others, or you may want to use different fonts or different layouts for different use cases. These choices are in the designer's hands. Tying your logic to some type of user benefit will create a more sustainable and meaningful system.

Carefully crafting the way you handle variations in the designs of your modules is your opportunity to affect the monotony in your designs.

Making Iterations

Iteration is about repeating a process on our design to get it closer and closer to satisfying goals through progressive improvements. We should be keeping our eye on the existing designs we have and constantly making them better as we get more data about our product.

Do you want higher click-throughs on your modules? Do you want users to reach further scroll depths? Maybe you want to increase time on the site? To figure out how we can optimize our designs to better at achieve these goals, we can apply an iterative approach to our modules.

The way we have set up our framework up to now gives us a solid foundation to work with. Not only can we use variations of our modules to achieve different tasks, but we can also use them to perform an iterative cycle. Figure 4-7 shows what this execution looks like within our framework.

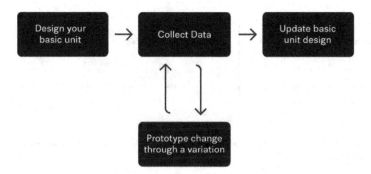

Figure 4-7. *What an iterative execution looks like in the way we've set up our design framework*

We can prototype alternative designs of our basic unit through a variation, gather data on it, and make a determination whether or not it is performing better than our original design. We keep doing this continuously to make sure our designs are as effective as they can be.

How can you tweak the design of your unit to advance those goals? Because we have established a modular system, improvements we make to our single module can have a compounding effect across our entire site. This is an extremely powerful characteristic of Modular Design Frameworks.

A/B Testing

Let's briefly go through the method of testing that will be the most effective in guiding your iterative process within this framework: A/B Testing. A/B testing is a method by which you show one design (version A) to a certain percentage of users and another design (version B) to the rest of your users. You then analyze a specific metric you are interested in about the designs, normalize the results, and compare them to each other to determine which design is best.

For example, say we want to test the existing design of our basic unit versus a new variation of it. We can show our existing design to 90% of our users, then the new design to other 10%. We often expose a much smaller percentage of users to new designs just in case the new design has a drastic negative impact on metrics. We reduce the amount of risk involved.

Modular Design Frameworks are excellent for A/B testing because you can easily interchange module variations to test against each other with little to no effort. Figure 4-8 is an example of how this could be executed just by simply applying a different class to the same markup.

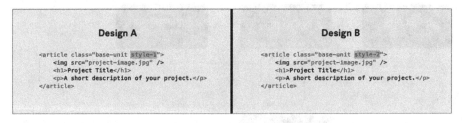

Figure 4-8. *An example of how two variations of the same base unit design can be applied in code that would make it easy to A/B test*

Let's go through a few simple examples of some design variations we can make to our modules for the purposes of iteration.

Example: Increase Click Rates

Let's say one of our objectives is to get more users to take action on our designs. We may have a hypothesis that we want our modules to appear more clickable. Let's add a button into our basic unit (Figure 4-9).

Figure 4-9. A variation on our basic unit, which adds a more visible button

This is a small change, and easily testable. If this gets applied across every unit throughout your site, it could have a huge impact with minimal to no effort at all.

You can even try different aesthetic variations to see if they'll have any type of impact. One simple aesthetic approach to try and affect the same exact metric would be to make the unit appear more clickable by applying a drop shadow (Figure 4-10).

NestFest

This poster was created to promote an end of the year barbeque.

Figure 4-10. *Applying a drop shadow to the card versus a pixel border to make it appear more clickable. Can it perform better? Let the metrics decide.*

As mentioned earlier in Chapter 1, aesthetics are all up to you; however, you now have the foundation to easily test different methods and have the data to back up design choices instead of debating over subjective preferences.

Example: Increase Scroll Depth

Are there ways we can use the design of our basic unit to get users to scroll further through our page? Using our framework we can test some simple variations, like playing with size and visual elements to guide the user further down the page (Figure 4-11).

Hello There!

My name is James and I am an award-winning
User Experience and Interface Designer based in
New York City.

NestFest

This poster was created to promote an end of
the year barbeque.

Figure 4-11. *Different design variation that affects size and introduces an arrow*

We can leverage our framework to rapidly implement and start measuring real
data from our users. We can observe the reactions to different designs to inform what
directions we should or shouldn't take. To many, this is a more effective approach than
spending time on ideological debates before even trying anything.

Summary

In this chapter we defined how we want to handle the way our Modular Design
Framework will adapt to various changes we may encounter. From our product needing
to accommodate new features, to optimizing with respect to certain metrics, we have
a plan for how we want to introduce alternative designs and update existing designs.
We see what we can reuse from our design, then we see how we can create variations of
existing designs, then we collect information on those variations and implement them
into our framework.

CHAPTER 5

■ ■ ■

Organization, Clustering, Pages, and Navigation

We now have the basis for our design framework through our basic unit and variations of that unit. What happens when we start putting our units together and composing more complicated layouts with them? Do they hold together or do they start to fall apart? In this chapter we will discuss various strategies for organizing, clustering, paging, and navigating through your base units.

Up until now we have only been focusing on the designs of the individual units. As far as using them to create larger layouts, we have only discussed the concept of flow from Chapter 2.

As we begin expanding our framework, we'll want to start mixing and matching our units to construct bigger modules. We're going to set you up with some ideas to consider as you form your designs.

Organization

As our content begins to grow we need to carefully think out how we want to organize everything. There are many ways to go about this, but we will just cover a few approaches so you can determine what's best for your product. The main point is that organization should be done primarily to facilitate your user's comprehension of your content.

Categorically

The most common way of organizing content is categorically. Typically under this model, your pieces of content will be divided under similar topics, themes, or properties.

© James Cabrera 2017
J. Cabrera, *Modular Design Frameworks*, DOI 10.1007/978-1-4842-1688-0_5

One of the most common examples of sites that get divided in this manner is Shopping sites. In Figure 5-1 we see a categorical breakdown of content on the Bloomingdale's site by Dresses, Active, Tops, Swimsuits, etc.

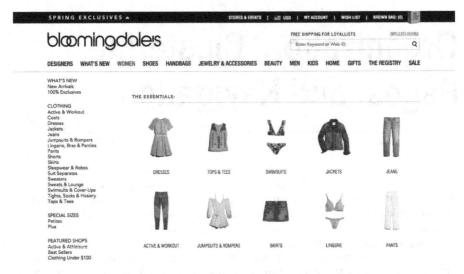

Figure 5-1. *Bloomingdale's women's section divided into deeper categories*

News and Media sites are also commonly organized under categories. In Figure 5-2 we take a look at The Verge, where they organize their content into categories like Tech, Science, Culture, and Cars.

Figure 5-2. The Verge is divided categorically as well

Consumption Paradigms

Suppose different pieces of your content can be consumed differently. A common example of this is articles vs. videos vs. audio. Articles need to be read, while videos can be played, and audio needs only to be listened to. This is a great way to separate your content out that will hugely benefit your users, because they don't require the same design.

In Figure 5-3 we look within the content of the design site It's Nice That to see that they have organized their content in a way that separates articles from videos. They have also given them different designs based on how they should be consumed.

Figure 5-3. It's Nice That separates articles from videos and gives them different design treatments

Make a decision on how you want to organize your content early on so you have an idea as to how you'll want to start guiding the expansion of designs within your own framework.

Clustering

Clustering is merely the simple act of creating a bigger module from a collection of base units. Figure 5-4 shows how a set of 16 base units can be reinterpreted as three bigger modules. These bigger modules are clusters.

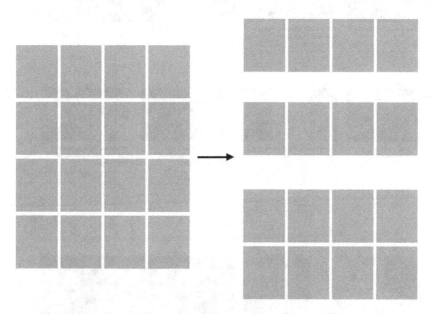

Figure 5-4. *We can form bigger modules by defining clusters of base units*

In clustering our units into bigger modules, we can start building bigger and better layouts. We'll have logical ways to separate out our content that makes sense for our users.

Media and Shopping Sites make the most use out of clustering since they always have a plethora of content they want to show the user. Clustering allows them to present their content in a clearer way.

In Figure 5-5 we see how Vice consciously clusters content to separate out their Latest Stories from their Video content.

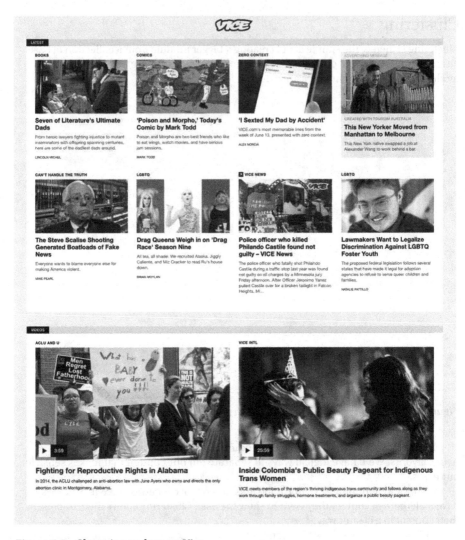

Figure 5-5. *Clustering as done on Vice*

In Figure 5-6 we also see an example of how Nike creates visual clusters to help their users parse through their products.

Figure 5-6. *Visual clusters for shoes, essentials, and brands, as seen on Nike's website*

As we think about our own Modular Design Framework potentially growing, we'll want to consider our own logic for how our units could be clustered together to form bigger modules. In considering my portfolio design from the previous chapter, Figure 5-7 shows how we might want to cluster it.

WEB DESIGN

phpProposal

phpProposal is an easy proposal creation product for independent contractors.

VIEW PROJECT

BeRaffled

BeRaffled was a digital product that allowed independent webmasters to easily run, manage and monitor giveaways.

VIEW PROJECT

PRINT WORK

NestFest

This poster was created to promote an end of the year barbeque.

VIEW PROJECT

Resume

This was my custom inforgraphic resume that I used from 2008-2011

VIEW PROJECT

Figure 5-7. *Applying the idea of clustering to my portfolio design from the previous chapter*

Designing with Cluster Modules

Now that we understand the basic idea of clustering, we want to try and design a finite set of cluster modules that we can begin reusing around our design. Imagine we have our basic unit A with a variation of that unit represented by B in Figure 5-8.

Figure 5-8. *Basic unit A with a variation unit B*

We then put these two units together to form a simple cluster module as seen in Figure 5-9.

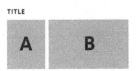

Figure 5-9. *Unit A and unit B put together into a cluster module*

Let's also make a second cluster module using three A units, as seen in Figure 5-10.

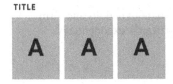

Figure 5-10. *Unit A used three times to design a cluster module*

We can then use the two separate cluster modules to start creating different design possibilities. Figure 5-11 shows just two layouts using these two-cluster modules. You can create many different layouts, with just this simple two-module, two-cluster construct.

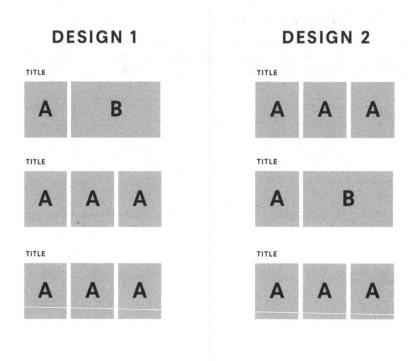

Figure 5-11. Unit A used three times to design a cluster module

This is just a very basic example. If you expand your variations of units and form different cluster modules with them, the possibilities begin to grow exponentially.

Paging

A more obvious way to expand on your framework is through paging your content. Paging is literally dividing out your content onto separate pages. Depending on how you've decided to organize your content will determine how you page your content.

Using your cluster modules, you can start composing templates for different types of pages. In Figure 5-12 we see that in Netflix's design, every category page shares the same template.

Figure 5-12. *Netflix Category Pages of Action & Adventure and Comedies*

If we were to achieve a similar design as Netflix's with our Modular Design Framework, we would need a single template that we could call a "Category Page" and have a majority of the site's design accounted for already.

When approaching your design framework, try to establish a limited number of templates to use across all of your pages.

To continue the example of my portfolio, I can think of two types of templates that I may need to compose page designs for the entire site, as represented in Figure 5-13.

PROJECT LIST

TITLE

| A | B |

TITLE

A	A	A
A	A	A
A	A	A

PROJECT DETAIL

TITLE

| A | B |

TITLE

C

Figure 5-13. *Project list and detail templates*

Navigational Design Elements

Now that we know how we want to organize, cluster, and page out our content, we should now consider how we want the user to navigate through it all. When we talk about the concept of navigation, menus may come to the top of mind.

With our Modular Design Framework, we want to change our perspective of navigation more toward the idea of sorting. As a user travels through the meat of your product, what they really want is an easy way to sort through it all to find what they're looking for. Navigational elements should facilitate how the user moves through various cluster modules and also across different pages.

Titles

Titles are an obvious piece of UI that will help us identify to the user the meanings of each of our pages and also clusters of content. As you may have noticed, this element was informally already added as seen in Figures 5-11 and 5-13. We can dress these up more aesthetically as we please.

Main Navigation

The Main Navigation is an important universal piece of UI that you should always include on every page of your design. This often includes branding for your page, along with a way to access a list of other pages in your design. Treat this like the remote control for the rest of your site (Figure 5-14).

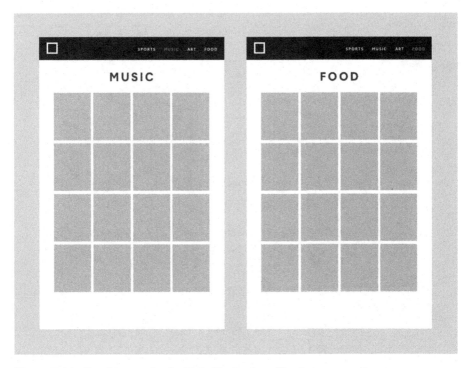

Figure 5-14. *Simple example of a Main Navigation affixed atop example pages*

Internal Filters

Filters are often an element seen mostly on Shopping Sites. However, filters could be great ways for a user to sort through the units in your modules to find exactly what they want. Consider incorporating filtering UI elements as part of your pages or even cluster modules.

In Figure 5-15 we show how Airbnb uses a filtering UI to help the user sort through the units on their Experiences page.

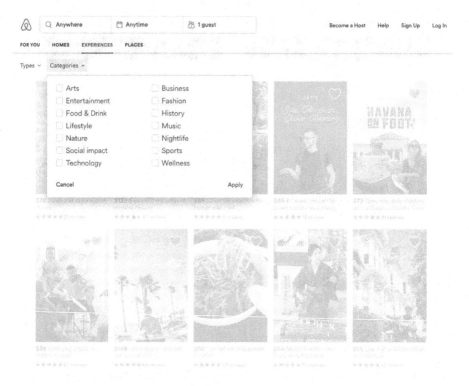

Figure 5-15. *Airbnb's filter UI on their Experiences page*

Breaking Down the Basic Unit

Although our basic unit should have been considered as our most fundamental piece of design, it is possible to also break it down further into submodules.

The common use case for this is to represent a small collection of content as a single unit. Maybe this comes in the form of a "popular content" module or maybe a multiple-part series of content (i.e., multiple-part tutorials, episodes of a show, multiple pieces of a single outfit, or breaking news stories). In Figure 5-16 we can see an example use case of this employed by Facebook for their Trending Topics module.

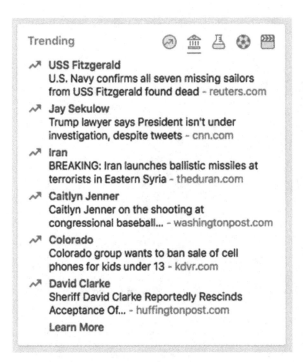

Figure 5-16. *The stories contained in this broken down module are just much smaller versions of posts you might also see appear as a regular unit in your feed*

If you have multiple pieces of content that are lower in hierarchy to whatever you've set as your basic unit, then you may need to create a design that breaks down your basic unit into smaller pieces. It's recommended not to go further than breaking down your unit one level down. Going any further will create modules that may be dramatically smaller in relative size to other groupings within your design. If you do believe you need to break it down further, then you may need to reconsider what you've decided for your basic unit (Figure 5-17).

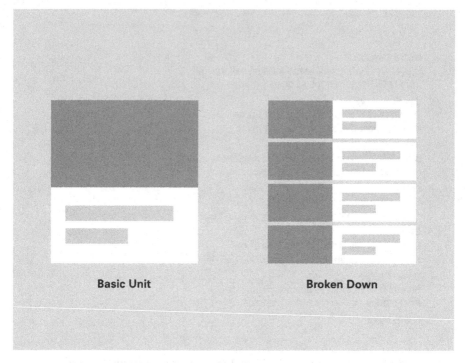

Figure 5-17. *An example breaking down of our basic unit*

Summary

In this chapter we outlined approaches on how to begin expanding your design framework from your basic units. We formed larger cluster modules from variations of basic units. We then created templates from compositions of cluster modules. With the addition of navigational UI elements to access all parts of the design, we now have all the foundational knowledge to design a complete framework on our own.

CHAPTER 6

■ ■ ■

What's Next?

At this point we have introduced the foundational pieces you need to consider when designing a Modular Design Framework of your own. What is outlined in this book is merely just the boilerplate of things you should consider when approaching your own designs.

If you craft your designs with an underlying logic utilizing these methods, you'll have much greater control when it comes to its implementation. The reason is because this approach in design is very similar to the approach taken when designing code. It's the act of building small reusable blocks that can be progressively enhanced to perform greater tasks. This method of design is just the visual representation of that concept, which is how design for digital should be handled.

Once we have laid our initial groundwork of basic units, variations, clusters, pages, and navigational elements, the job from here is to continually enhance each of those pieces. What new features will your product need to add in the future? What metrics do you want to improve upon? These are only a couple questions that you can attack with easy updates to your framework.

Each and every piece of your system is impermanent, meaning that you should be able to quickly modify, redesign, or tweak any part without requiring any huge overhaul of the entire design. Since everything is based off of your repeatable modules, you can affect change rapidly and at scale. These changes will also be specific to the habits and behaviors of your user's unique experience with your product.

Let's go back through each of the major concepts of your Modular Design Framework and look at what could potentially be next as far as evolving and maintaining the design language of your framework for your product.

Fonts, Colors, and the Invisible UI

Many brands, especially those that are not yet established, and constantly looking for ways to stand out, may go through several brand overhauls in their lifetimes. For your modular framework, the ability to update the design to accommodate completely different branding elements should be just as easy as reassigning new font files and new color codes to only a few different variables.

You may want to add more fonts or add additional logic by way of additional variables. Our original example only included headline, body, and UI fonts, when your system can expand based on your content to include things such as a meta-information font, caption font, citation font, or whatever your product might require based on your content. It really is ultimately up to you how you wish to construct your system.

© James Cabrera 2017

J. Cabrera, *Modular Design Frameworks*, DOI 10.1007/978-1-4842-1688-0_6

The same goes for colors and assigning new hex codes to only a few existing variables. If anything, you may want to add some complexity to your color system to make your designs a little more dynamic and not as predictable. For example, you might want to implement a random color scheme into your color system, or leverage techniques like using dominant colors from images to fill containers.

You may want to consider how and if you can implement your chosen fonts and colors for your product on other platforms. If you can't use custom color values or import typefaces, you may need to determine system/platform-based fonts and color fallback rules. For example, you only have access to a limited amount of typefaces on iOS, which are also different on Android, and Windows-based systems. Since the convention we established on applying fonts and colors is based off of a naming system dependent on functional usage (headline, body, UI, etc.), and a color naming system based on relative hierarchy (primary, secondary), it ultimately does not matter as much what the actual values are so we can ensure our design stays relatively consistent no matter where it appears.

As new platforms emerge that you need to adapt your product onto, you should always be optimizing and evolving your core framework, and not simply making offshoots of your design.

For screenless interfaces you may need to employ elements like language and brand-voice into your framework. This may be done by establishing tone rules in your copywriting.

The Basic Unit

Whether you're building a product from scratch or creating a new system for an existing product, your basic unit will require an endless amount of attention. Since your basic unit represents your absolute core set of data, all of your future work involves maintaining that data. That includes adjusting the design to either take into account more data, or finding ways to strip out data that's been tested and verified to be excess.

As your product develops and evolves through time, you'll encounter several requests to always add more and more to your design. As the designer, you'll need to be the gatekeeper of what core set of data you choose to expose within your basic unit. You should constantly be playing with various elements, determining what is and isn't important to include as potential elements to manipulate and display.

Variations, Optimizations, and iterations

Similarly to maintaining the data for your basic unit, maintaining your inventory of variations of your basic unit is just as important. Having too many variations may visually clutter any type of hierarchy you hope to establish, while not having enough variations will keep your design flat and unfocused.

Since you have a modular system, the biggest advantage is your ability to quickly swap in and out design changes at scale. For this reason you should constantly be testing and analyzing different variations before solidifying them as part of the system.

The technological landscape is fickle, and sometimes data that you've gathered to prove or disprove certain design decisions could change in a matter of months or even weeks. For this reason you should constantly be collecting and analyzing data on variations of your designs to know whether or not something needs to be tweaked or replaced.

In some cases, even the functionality of your product may drastically change, causing you to completely redesign your basic unit and variations of it. These are things to be completely aware of and to constantly stay on top of as a designer of the framework.

You may also want to work on adding complexity into the relationships between variations of your modules. If your product has significantly developed from its early stage, you may need to deliver on complicated features, which require more logic from your system. You will need to constantly adapt, improve, and iterate on your design framework in a smart way in order to maintain its sustainability. This can be done through proper management and development of your framework's variations, iterations, and optimizations.

Clusters, Pages, and Navigation

Your cluster modules and page compositions will likely be greatly affected by any updates you make to your basic units and variations. So your most important task here is to make sure the logic you've established holds up as you continue to progressively make changes. If you need to introduce new design elements, you should make sure they can easily be accommodated.

Your cluster modules and pages may even serve to accomplish certain tasks themselves. So you may want to apply testing to these compositions as well to inform their designs.

A Never-Ending Job

Maintaining your framework is a never-ending job. It's a constant cycle of experimenting new things, adding functionality, and feeding all of your new learnings back into the system. Sometimes you may also need to tear down and reconstruct parts of the system.

This methodology is merely just a way to set you up for the right type of thinking when approaching your own projects. It's not a process that needs to be followed religiously, since you have a lot of freedom as far as setting up your own visual language and deciding exactly what you want to display, and how it gets displayed. This is an approach to how to structure your design in a way that can easily manifest itself for your own purposes.

Hopefully, after reading this book you'll have a new perspective on how to approach the way you design products. The next time you go into a project, try to apply this line of thinking to your compositions, and make a framework out of it.

Summary

Don't ever assume that whatever design you create is ever complete or final. Design should be organic, growing alongside your product. The most successful digital products have gone a long way design-wise since from when they first launched. Just think about how many times Facebook users were outraged because of a design update. Designing with change in mind from the start will save you a lot of work in the long run. So keep collecting data, keep testing changes, and keep evolving the design using your framework.

■ ■ ■

Breaking Down Examples into Modular Systems

One of the biggest criticisms of Modular Design systems is that the designs are always bland and uniform. While many actually applied systems might appear that way, that doesn't need to be the case. It also shouldn't be the case once there are more designers who fully understand the proper way to logically design for these systems.

In fact, I might be able to argue that any site can be theoretically broken down into a modularly defined system, whether or not they actually built it with a modular structure in mind. This Appendix will take you through visually diverse examples of live sites, and how those designs could be broken down into a modular as outlined in this book.

The goal here is to continue to inspire you to always make an effort to define a modular structure and logic underneath your creative layouts.

Example 1: Herokid Studios

Herokid Studios is a creative services company who has a pretty slick and minimal design for their site. The design in Figure A-1 can be easily achieved with the logic of a simple Modular Design Framework.

J. Cabrera, *Modular Design Frameworks*, DOI 10.1007/978-1-4842-1688-0

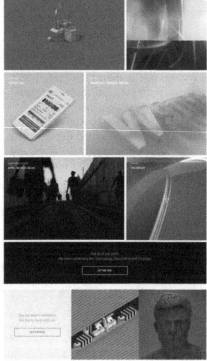

Figure A-1. *A screenshot of Herokid Studios' site design*

Font System

While it seems like Herokid Studios only uses two type styles, it's still important to create a font system defined by functions. For this design, it appears we can establish a system with three fonts: A **Title Font**, a **Client Label Font**, and a **Reading Font**.

A **Title Font** is seen to be used for the main subject line of each module and is using the typeface *Nuzeit Grotesk Uppercase* (Figure A-2).

Figure A-2. *Close-up examples of titles on Herokid Studios' site*

A **Client Label Font** can be defined in this design for all of the labels marking whom a particular project was done for. The typeface used for this is *Roboto Uppercase* (Figure A-3).

Figure A-3. *Close-up examples of the client labels on Herokid Studios' site*

The last of the font styles needed to compose a font system around Herokid's site is a **Reading Font**. The Reading Font appears to be used in areas that provide more context for each piece of content, and is simply using *Roboto* (Figure A-4).

Figure A-4. *Close-up examples of descriptions on Herokid Studios' site*

Base Unit

The design of the base unit here is quite simple. It's a block with an image background and a couple of blocks of text atop it and a call-to-action (Figure A-5).

73

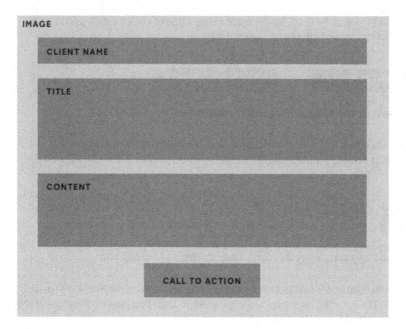

Figure A-5. *A way to reinterpret Herokid Studios' design from a basic unit under our modular design strategy*

The **flow** for the units is a normal Z pattern, going from left to right then wrapping down to the next row.

Variations

You might notice this base unit looks like it has way too much on it compared to the actual blocks in the design. That's because we want our base unit to incorporate every possible piece that could be displayed. Any element that is not used is easily hidden.

Let's see how this base unit takes on different forms throughout the design. Figure A-6 shows a few of the modules from the page side by side with the base unit to see how it adapts. For each unit, what's highlighted in green is what's being used and in red is what's being hidden.

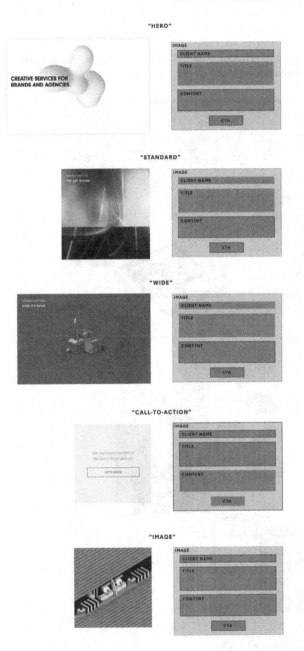

Figure A-6. *A way we could define the rest of the Herokid Studios' design as variations of our proposed basic unit*

Example 2: Huge

Huge is a much bigger, well-known international digital creative agency, and has a strong design sense (Figure A-7). Let's take a look at the design for their site.

Figure A-7. *A screenshot of Huge's site design*

Font System

It appears that Huge uses a fairly simple logical font system. It can likely be broken down and defined into three types: a **Headline Font**, **Label Font**, and **Reading Font**.

The **Headline Font** is used wherever there are big and bold titles for content and is using the typeface *Avante Garde Bold* (Figure A-8).

What It Means to Be a Smart Brand in the Age of AI.

What AI Means For Marketers.

Figure A-8. *A close-up example of titles within Huge's design*

The **Label Font** appears to be used wherever there is meta information associated to a piece of content and the typeface being used is *Arial* (Figure A-9).

IDEAS / Perspective

IDEAS / Video

Figure A-9. *A close-up example of meta information within Huge's design*

Finally, the **Reading Font** is used for the actual content itself that gives context. It's used for the article abstracts as well as the body copy and is in the typeface *Galaxie Copernicus Book* (Figure A-10).

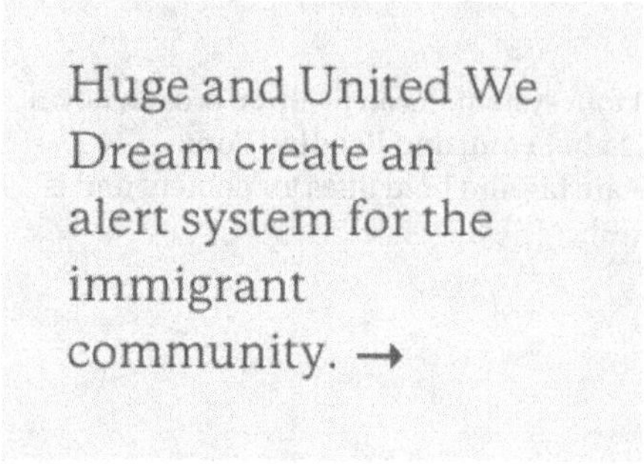

Huge and United We Dream create an alert system for the immigrant community. →

Figure A-10. *A close-up example of article abstracts within Huge's design*

Base Unit

Huge's design can be based off of a pretty flexible single base unit (Figure A-11).

IMAGE
LABEL
HEADLINE
ABSTRACT
IDEAS / Perspective
Key Principles for High-Performing Engineering Teams.

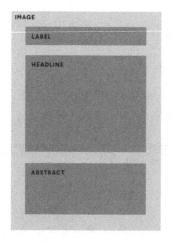

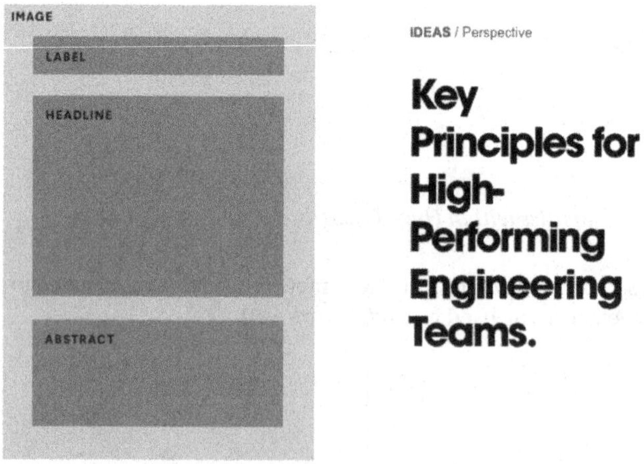

Figure A-11. *A way to reinterpret Huge's design from a basic unit under our modular design strategy*

You may question if the Abstract is actually part of the base unit since it is almost nowhere to be found. That's because in most cases it is omitted; however, it is required for other areas of the design, which you'll see later. As part of your base unit design it is better to include everything and omit pieces for variations than to conditionally add pieces for variations.

The **flow** of the units is a *waterfall*. A *waterfall* is a slightly more complex version of a Z pattern. A *waterfall* moves left to right, then down to the closest available spot vertically since each unit has a variable height based on the amount of content within it. Figure A-12 provides an example to understand this unit flow.

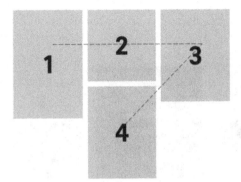

Figure A-12. *Diagram illustrating the flow of cards within Huge's design*

As you can see the unit 4 flows below unit 2 since that is the next available position, vertically, as opposed to below unit 1.

Variations

There are several variations of the base unit being used by Huge. Figure A-13 show some different examples and just exactly how they are variations of the basic unit by outlining in green what is being, and outlining in red what's just being hidden.

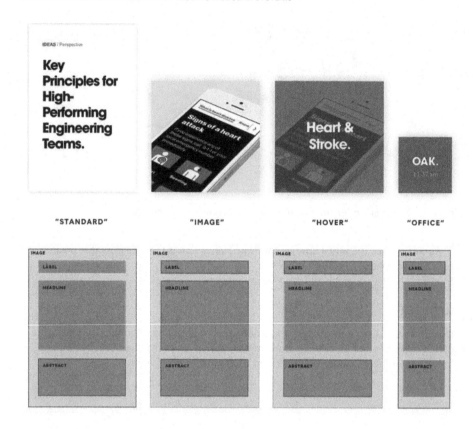

Figure A-13. *A way we could define the rest of Huge's design as variations of our proposed basic unit*

Example 3: iPhone 7

Let's take a look at a slightly different design, focused on an individual product, the iPhone7 (Figure A-14). While Apple is highly regarded as a design-centric company, we'll see that the design of their sites that are marketing their products are actually quite simple if we follow our modular design approach.

Figure A-14. *A screenshot of Apple's iPhone 7 site design*

Font System

Since introducing their new San Francisco typeface, Apple has been applying it everywhere in their products. Their font system ends up being very simple, and also semantic. In trying to break this design down into a designed system, it seems to follow that we can use conventional HTML as inspiration with a **Headline Font**, **Sub Headline Font**, **Paragraph Font**, and **Link Font**.

While all fonts all use San Francisco with a slight alteration in font weight, we still need to separate out the application of the fonts by function, for future sustainability of the design system (Figure A-15).

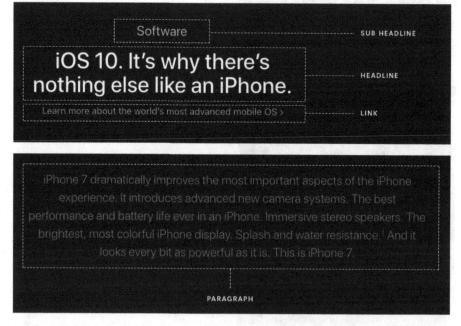

Figure A-15. *Breaking down Apple's iPhone 7 site design to create a potential font system*

Base Unit

The base unit on the iPhone7 site is also quite simple and familiar (Figure A-16).

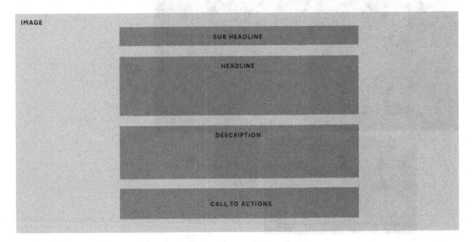

Figure A-16. *A way to reinterpret Huge's design from a basic unit under our modular design strategy*

The **flow** of the units is directly from the top-down.

Variations

There is barely any variation necessary to the design of the base unit to achieve the iPhone7 design. Everything can follow from nearly the same design, aside from a video module and a detail module (Figure A-17).

Figure A-17. Examples from Apple's iPhone 7 page showing what could be variations of the same unit under our modular design strategy

One in the Same

You may notice in the analysis of how these three seemingly different examples can be built using a modularly designed system, which they may all follow the same exact framework. This is exactly true. Of course there are sights that can leverage a differently designed basic unit; however, the majority of what modern sites and applications require at the onset is one in the same design.

That's the power of designing the system versus designing just based on aesthetic. As a designer we can design the framework, then just by simply modifying the rules of the system we can easily transform the look and feel of a site like Huge into the design of that of the iPhone7.

There are other ways to architect your base unit, and this is where your creativity as a designer comes into play: thinking out of the box, as the saying goes. Also, being able to A/B test variations of your base unit to help you settle on your final design would be advantageous.

Designing for the framework versus designing just the pixels arbitrarily will allow you to create much more sustainable designs that can be handled automatically by code. Instead of requiring production designers to create mocks, design updates can be down instantly on the fly with just a few programmatic tweaks.

Index

© James Cabrera 2017
J. Cabrera, *Modular Design Frameworks*, DOI 10.1007/978-1-4842-1688-0

Get the eBook for only $5!

Why limit yourself?

With most of our titles available in both PDF and ePUB format, you can access your content wherever and however you wish—on your PC, phone, tablet, or reader.

Since you've purchased this print book, we are happy to offer you the eBook for just $5.

To learn more, go to http://www.apress.com/companion or contact support@apress.com.

Apress®

Printed in the United States
By Bookmasters